GOING TO WAR IN
VIKING TIMES

GOING TO WAR IN
VIKING TIMES

CHRISTOPHER GRAVETT

W
FRANKLIN WATTS
A Division of Grolier Publishing
NEW YORK • LONDON • HONG KONG • SYDNEY
DANBURY, CONNECTICUT

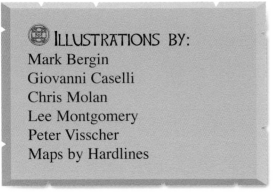

ILLUSTRATIONS BY:
Mark Bergin
Giovanni Caselli
Chris Molan
Lee Montgomery
Peter Visscher
Maps by Hardlines

Editor Penny Clarke
Editor-in-Chief John C. Miles
Designer Steve Prosser
Art Director Jonathan Hair

First published in 2000 by
Franklin Watts
96 Leonard Street
London
EC2A 4XD

First American edition 2001 by Franklin Watts
A Division of Grolier Publishing
90 Sherman Turnpike
Danbury, CT 06816

Catalog details are available from the Library of
Congress Cataloging-in-Publication Data

Visit Franklin Watts on the internet at:
http://publishing.grolier.com

ISBN   0-531-14592-1 (lib.bdg)
        0-531-16353-9 (pbk)

GROLIER
PUBLISHING

CONTENTS

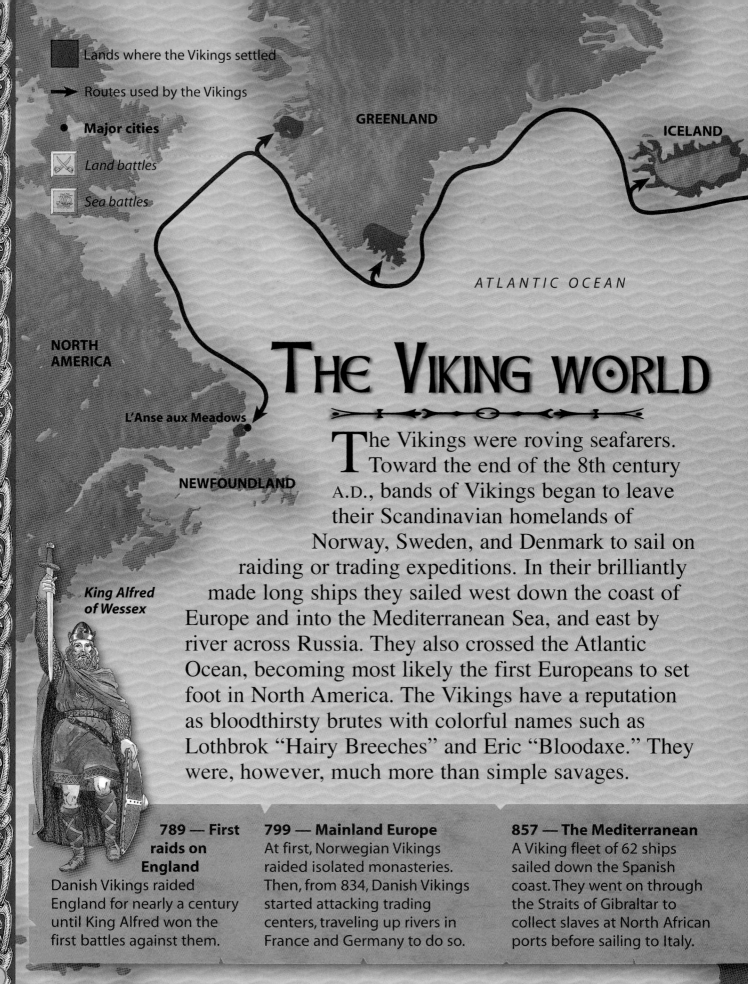

Lands where the Vikings settled

→ Routes used by the Vikings

● **Major cities**

⚔ Land battles

🚢 Sea battles

GREENLAND

ICELAND

ATLANTIC OCEAN

NORTH
AMERICA

L'Anse aux Meadows

NEWFOUNDLAND

*King Alfred
of Wessex*

THE VIKING WORLD

The Vikings were roving seafarers. Toward the end of the 8th century A.D., bands of Vikings began to leave their Scandinavian homelands of Norway, Sweden, and Denmark to sail on raiding or trading expeditions. In their brilliantly made long ships they sailed west down the coast of Europe and into the Mediterranean Sea, and east by river across Russia. They also crossed the Atlantic Ocean, becoming most likely the first Europeans to set foot in North America. The Vikings have a reputation as bloodthirsty brutes with colorful names such as Lothbrok "Hairy Breeches" and Eric "Bloodaxe." They were, however, much more than simple savages.

789 — First raids on England
Danish Vikings raided England for nearly a century until King Alfred won the first battles against them.

799 — Mainland Europe
At first, Norwegian Vikings raided isolated monasteries. Then, from 834, Danish Vikings started attacking trading centers, traveling up rivers in France and Germany to do so.

857 — The Mediterranean
A Viking fleet of 62 ships sailed down the Spanish coast. They went on through the Straits of Gibraltar to collect slaves at North African ports before sailing to Italy.

A. Battle of Ashdown 871
   and Battle of Edington 878
B. Battle of Maldon 981
C. Battle of Clontarf 1014
D. Battle of Hastings 1066

FAEROE ISLANDS

SHETLAND ISLANDS

Stiklestad 1030

SCANDINAVIA

NORWAY   SWEDEN

Hafrsfjord c. 890

● **Kaupang**

SCOTLAND

● **Lindisfarne**

Brunanburh 937

● **Aggersborg**

DENMARK

IRELAND

Dublin

London

B.

● **Hedeby**

C.

D.

Dorestad

A.

Saucourt 881

Dyle 891

St. Lô 890

Paris

Rheims 882

FRANKISH EMPIRE

SPAIN

● **Pisa**
● **Rome**

ITALY

● **Seville**

● **Piraeus**

Constantinople ●

RUSSIA

● **Novgorod**

● **Kiev**

BLACK SEA

CASPIAN SEA

BYZANTINE EMPIRE

860 — Vikings in Russia

Swedish Vikings sailed to Novgorod along the Russian rivers. This Resurrection egg, Christian symbol of rebirth, was among the things they brought back.

Byzantine stone lion carved with Viking graffiti and found in Greece

MEDITERRANEAN SEA

● **Baghdad**

● **Jerusalem**

860 Constantinople

After attacking Constantinople, capital of the Byzantine Empire, many Vikings joined the Varangian Guard — the emperor's bodyguard.

970 — Iceland

From Shetland and the Faeroe Islands north of Scotland, the Vikings sailed west and came to Iceland. The only people living there were a small number of Irish monks.

981 — Greenland

From Iceland, some Vikings sailed to Greenland. This axe is made from whalebone, like Inuit weapons. By about A.D. 1000 Vikings reached North America.

Armor and Weapons

Most Vikings probably wore little armor and just went into battle in their ordinary clothes. They wore a knee-length tunic and trousers or hose, a type of long thick leggings. On their feet were sturdy shoes or boots. A thick cloak held by a pin or brooch protected them from the cold.

If a warrior wore body armor, it was because he was rich. Those who could not afford mail probably used reindeer skins or cowhide. But rich or poor, a warrior's lower arms and legs had little protection from his enemies' slashing swords.

⊛ ARMOR

Before battle, a wealthy warrior put on his coat of mail made from thousands of interlinked iron rings. The coat reached to his hips or knees and had sleeves down to the elbows. A round or cone-shaped helmet completed his armor.

⊛ WEAPONS

Viking warriors valued their swords more than any other weapon. Swords used by the bravest fighters had almost legendary reputations. Vikings also fought with axes, but these were never as highly prized as swords. Throwing or thrusting spears and a knife in a leather sheath completed a Viking warrior's weapons. Archers fought with wooden bows $6^1/_2$ feet (2 meters) high.

Axe

Helmet

Cloak

Shield

Cloak pin

Mail armor

Tunic

Sword

Leather shoes

ARMS AND ARMOR

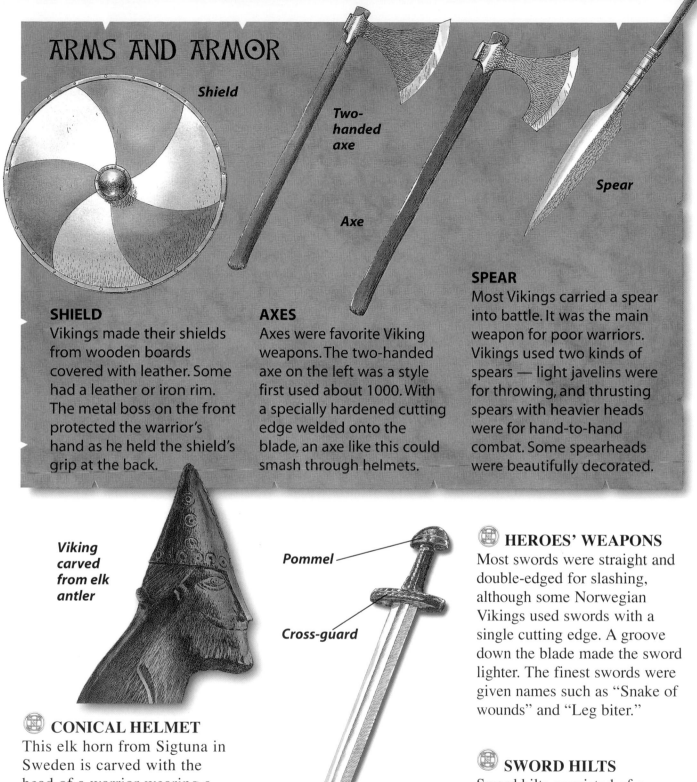

Shield

Two-handed axe

Axe

Spear

SHIELD
Vikings made their shields from wooden boards covered with leather. Some had a leather or iron rim. The metal boss on the front protected the warrior's hand as he held the shield's grip at the back.

AXES
Axes were favorite Viking weapons. The two-handed axe on the left was a style first used about 1000. With a specially hardened cutting edge welded onto the blade, an axe like this could smash through helmets.

SPEAR
Most Vikings carried a spear into battle. It was the main weapon for poor warriors. Vikings used two kinds of spears — light javelins were for throwing, and thrusting spears with heavier heads were for hand-to-hand combat. Some spearheads were beautifully decorated.

Viking carved from elk antler

Pommel

Cross-guard

Double-edged Viking sword

⊙ HEROES' WEAPONS
Most swords were straight and double-edged for slashing, although some Norwegian Vikings used swords with a single cutting edge. A groove down the blade made the sword lighter. The finest swords were given names such as "Snake of wounds" and "Leg biter."

⊙ CONICAL HELMET
This elk horn from Sigtuna in Sweden is carved with the head of a warrior wearing a conical helmet with a nose-guard. Most Viking helmets were probably like this.

The helmets with wings and horns sometimes seen in films were not used, although horned helmets may have been made for religious ceremonies.

⊙ SWORD HILTS
Sword hilts consisted of a cross-guard to protect the hand, a grip, and a weighted end, or pommel. The iron hilts of swords belonging to wealthy Vikings were decorated with tin, silver, brass, copper, or even gold — the elaborate decoration was a status symbol.

WARRIORS AND SOCIETY

At the beginning of the Viking period, Scandinavia was ruled by many chieftains. Each one held power in a small area, backed by a band of warriors who would fight (and die) for him. Slowly, more ruthless chieftains took over the lands of their neighbors until by about 1050 a single king ruled each country.

Viking society also included farmers, merchants, and craftsmen, who were all free people. Landless peasants and thralls (slaves) worked for the free members of society.

THE THING

"Things" were assemblies that usually lasted for several days. They were a combination of law court and parliament, where disputes and other matters were decided. There were small local Things and larger, more important, regional ones. Only freemen could attend the Things.

Chieftain addressing a Thing

REWARDS

Viking warriors expected their chieftain to reward them well with land and the spoils of their battles. If he didn't, they might desert him for another chieftain who promised better rewards. Among the warriors, an elite group, the "lith," lived with the chieftain in his hall as his close retainers. When each Scandinavian country became a single kingdom, it was subdivided into small units. Each unit had to provide a warrior to fight for the king.

FIGHTING DUELS

Fighting a duel was the usual way Vikings settled their differences. *Holmganga*, a Viking word for "duel," actually means "island going," perhaps because fighting the duel on a small island meant there would be little interference. The Vikings' practice of fighting duels on a piece of cloth may have developed from this, with the cloth representing the island.

FEUDS

Viking warriors were always ready to avenge wrongs done to members of their family. When someone was killed illegally, the murderer and his kinsmen all had to pay "blood money" to the victim's family.

If a warrior stepped off the cloth, he lost the duel.

HEROES

Sigurd
Sigurd is one of many legendary Viking heroes. This carving shows Regin forging a sword for Sigurd to slay the dragon Fafnir.

Sagas
Sagas were stories about Viking gods and heroes. They were told by skalds (poets) on dark winter evenings. Sagas were eventually written down in manuscripts like the one in which this painting appears.

Viking coins
Many foreign coins reached Scandinavia through trade, plunder, or as bribes paid by harassed kings to get rid of the Vikings. Eventually the Vikings made their own coins bearing the heads of famous kings, such as this one showing Cnut, King of Denmark and England.

WHY VIKINGS WENT RAIDING

W hy did the Vikings erupt from their homelands in the late 8th century, leave their mark on half the world, then disappear a few hundred years later? There were probably several reasons. Norway and Sweden, in particular, are mountainous, with the best farming land along the coasts. This meant that there was very little room for families to expand.

Where a population became too large, people might leave to seek new homes across the sea. Others used their seafaring skills to trade far and wide, but found that raiding was easier and more profitable.

Shipbuilders at work

TRADE

Viking merchants sailed to many foreign ports. They traded in walrus ivory for ornaments and boxes; furs for clothing and bedding; as well as timber, Baltic amber, falcons, and slaves.

A Norwegian Viking settlement

RAIDING AND SETTLING

As time went on, the Vikings became increasingly eager to hold on to the lands they had won, rather than just living by raiding.

As a result, many Vikings stayed and settled in their newly conquered territory. One such region was the part of England known as the Danelaw, where the Vikings lived as traders or farmers.

COLONIZATION

Viking men and women settled in new lands, such as the Orkney and Shetland Islands, the Isle of Man, Iceland, Greenland, and northern France. They built homes and raised families.

Sometimes the settlers traded with local people living nearby; sometimes they fought them. Some settlements were very successful; others, such as those in Greenland where the climate is very harsh, were eventually abandoned.

The narrow, sheltered waters of fjords were good for ships.

A raiding party gets ready to sail.

On soft ground the Vikings surfaced their roads with planks.

Viking towns were cramped — animals and people lived close together.

13

LONG SHIPS

Viking shipbuilders were extremely skilled. The long ships they built were primarily warships, but they were strong enough for long voyages of exploration. They carried Vikings as far as the Mediterranean Sea and across the Atlantic Ocean to North America.

The largest-known long ship was 92 feet (28 meters) long and carried 200 to 300 warriors. Many vessels had an impressive carved figurehead on the bow (front) representing the head of a dragon or some other animal.

Long ships were so shallow they could also sail close to the shore.

LONG SHIP LAYOUT

With one large sail to catch the wind and oars for rowing when necessary, long ships could navigate almost anywhere.

They were completely open — spreading a tent over the deck was the only protection for those on board. There was no seating, so when using the oars the rowers sat on the chests that held their personal possessions.

Shields could be hung along the sides of the ship for display or to give a little protection from the waves, or when in battle.

LONG SHIP DESIGN

Hull of a long ship

SAILS AND RIGGING
Few details of long ships' rigging have survived, although it was probably fairly simple.

A long diagonal wooden spar at one corner of the sail allowed the crew to fine-tune the ship's sailing performance.

HULLS
Viking ships were clinker built. This means that they were made from overlapping planks. These were fastened by nails or wooden pegs; gaps were sealed with tarred rope, or caulking.

Boats built like this have hulls that can flex slightly and withstand rough seas because they are not rigid. Long ships did not sit deep in the water and could go into shallow water without running aground.

RUDDERS

The helmsman steered a long ship with a steering oar attached to the right side. From this comes the term starboard ("steer-board") for the right-hand side of a ship.

TRADING SHIPS

Viking seafarers also used a deeper-bodied ship, the knorr. Because of their shape, knorrs were slower than long ships; they also had fewer oars.

Their deep bodies made knorrs ideal for deep-sea trading runs or transporting families to new lands. Not only was there much more room for supplies, but they could also be used for carrying livestock — horses could jump from ships when necessary.

As well as long ships and knorrs, the Vikings had smaller boats they used for short journeys up and down the coast of their homelands.

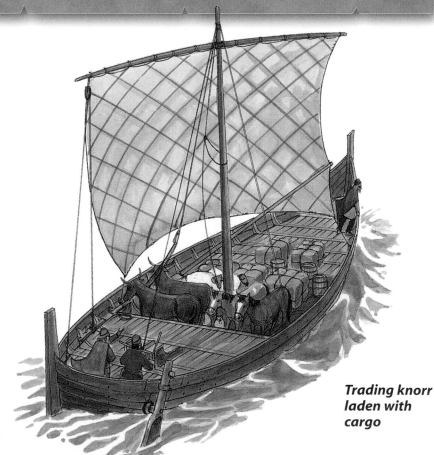

Trading knorr laden with cargo

NAVAL BATTLES AND RAIDS

The Vikings often feuded and fought with each other. They liked to fight their naval battles in the sheltered waters of a fjord, where it was easy for the long ships to row toward each other.

Sometimes ships were lashed together to make a large platform on which to fight. Iron frames fixed to the ships' bows acted as rams or stopped enemy warriors from boarding. Eventually the Vikings decided raiding on land was more profitable than fighting battles at sea.

BATTLE OF SVÖLDR

The saga of King Olaf Tryggvasson describes this sea battle, which took place in 1000. Olaf's ship, *Long Serpent,* was surrounded by his enemies' ships. The air was thick with flying arrows and javelins. Angered by the barrage, Olaf's men tried to leap onto the enemies' ships. But most of the ships were just beyond reach, and many of the men fell overboard and drowned. Eventually, surrounded by enemies who had boarded *Long Serpent*, Olaf jumped into the sea and drowned rather than let himself be taken prisoner.

⊕ RIVER RAIDS

All over Europe, rivers such as the Rhine, the Seine, and the Loire provided highways for Viking raiders. The shallow long ships could be rowed quickly up the rivers. As a result, the Vikings could strike deep into the heart of a country and be off again before any resistance could be organized.

⊕ ROWING UP THE SEINE

With sail furled and mast lowered (above), Vikings row their long ship up the River Seine in France on the way to raid the wealthy city of Paris.

RAIDS

ATTACK ON LINDISFARNE

The monastery on the island of Lindisfarne off the coast of northeast England was renowned for its learning. Christian Europe was shocked when it was sacked by Norwegian Vikings in 793.

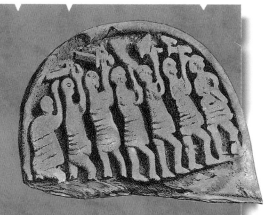

LOOTERS AND RAIDERS

Undefended religious houses, with their tempting prizes of gold and precious objects, provided rich pickings for armed Viking warriors. Poorly defended towns and villages (above) were also easy targets.

LINDISFARNE STONE

This stone may be a grave marker made after the attack of 793. It is carved in Viking style and shows Viking warriors waving axes and swords. No one knows if it was made by an English craftsman or a Viking.

LAND BATTLES

Even Vikings wealthy enough to ride to battle fought on foot. Each chieftain had his chosen fighting men around him. But the Vikings' forces were small. Even the Danish Great Army, which had a ferocious reputation, may have numbered less than a thousand men.

Battles began with the exchange of arrows, javelins, and insults. Then the two sides closed in for vicious hand-to-hand combat. Neither side showed any mercy.

RAVEN BANNER
Vikings fought under the banners of their chieftains. On some of these banners was a raven, the bird associated with the god Odin.

Earl Sigurd of Orkney had a banner that, when it fluttered, looked like a raven in flight. According to legend, if the banner drooped, Earl Sigurd's men would be defeated.

Defeated Vikings mourn their dead.

BEAR-SHIRTS AND WOLFSKINS
The *berserkirs*, or "bear-shirts," were warriors dedicated to Odin. They usually wore a bearskin and often threw off their armor, working themselves into a frenzy so that they would feel no pain. Kings often had groups of *berserkirs* in their bodyguard. A similar type of warrior was the *ulfhednar*, or "wolfskin-clad one." By wearing skins and howling, these warriors probably believed they took on the animal's ferocity.

VIKING TACTICS

SHIELD FORT

A line of overlapping shields, the *skjaldborg,* or "shield fort," was a strong temporary defense. The warriors in front knelt to protect the legs of those behind. They might wait like this, holding off the enemy, until reinforcements came.

ISLAND STRONGHOLDS

About 860 a Viking fleet reached a small island in the River Seine, several miles from Paris, and made camp, safe from the Frankish army on both banks. In hostile territory, islands made excellent, easily defended camps.

BURHS

To capture fortified places, the Vikings used siege tactics and equipment such as scaling ladders. Here they attack an English "burh," a large enclosure surrounded by a ditch, banks, and timber palisade (fence).

King Alfred of Wessex

KING ALFRED

Alfred of Wessex won his first battle against the Danish Vikings at Ashdown in 871 when he charged "like a wild boar" and routed the enemy.

In 878 the Danes caught him off guard and he fled to west Wessex. But he regrouped his forces and beat the Danish Viking leader, Guthrum, at Edington. This victory saved all of England from becoming a Danish kingdom.

Map showing the Danelaw and neighboring kingdoms

Scotland

Ireland

Welsh Kings

West Welsh

Wessex

UNITED FORCES

Unable to defeat Alfred, the Danes settled in the area known as the Danelaw. In 937 a Celtic-Norse invasion was beaten at Brunanburh. England was finally conquered by Danes led by King Cnut in 1014, in a second wave of Viking attacks.

VIKINGS GO WEST

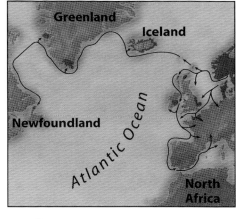

Although Vikings preferred to sail within sight of land, it was not long before they ventured into the North Sea. Their first raid on England was in the late 8th century. This was soon followed by many others.

Vikings descended on Scotland, Ireland, France, Germany, and the Netherlands. Moving down the coast to Spain and North Africa, they sailed through the Straits of Gibraltar into the Mediterranean Sea, to Italy and beyond.

Meanwhile, other Vikings settled in Iceland and other groups sailed on to Greenland, where they probably encountered the Inuit people. From here some ships explored even farther west, discovering the coast of North America.

SAILING WEST

In the 9th century, Norwegian Vikings made sea voyages via the Scottish islands and reached a wild place they named Iceland (above). From here, about 981, Erik the Red sailed on to Greenland — he hoped the name would attract settlers. His son, Leif, explored the coast of Newfoundland.

 HELD TO RANSOM
When Viking attacks became really bad, harassed kings sometimes paid *Danegeld*, large sums of money to buy off the attackers. This never really solved the problem; the Vikings simply returned later for more.

 STONE WALLS
London was attacked several times but was still protected by its old Roman walls (right). In 994, Danish Vikings tried to burn the city but were driven off. In 1016 Cnut of Denmark, finding his ships blocked by London Bridge, dug a channel to drag them around it, but still failed to capture London.

CITY DEFENSES

Some towns and cities were protected by ditches or stone walls, but these did not always keep the Vikings out.

In 845 a Viking called Ragnar attacked and sacked Paris, despite its walls. In 857, it was sacked again. In 885-886, troops from a great fleet of about 700 ships attacked yet again, using pickaxes, fire, siege towers, and catapults. The Vikings filled the ditches and attacked using a *testudo,* or "tortoise," a formation in which they advanced while holding their shields over their heads.

THE VIKINGS IN NORTH AMERICA

Leif Eriksson had called his new discovery Vinland ("Wineland") after the grapes (probably actually huckleberries) that grew there. Traces left by Viking settlers led by Thorfinn Karlsefni have been found at L'Anse aux Meadows in Newfoundland. There was plenty of food, and the newcomers appear to have traded with the locals, probably native Americans, whom they called *skraelings,* or "savages." However, the natives soon realized that they were being exploited by the new arrivals, and fighting broke out. After three years, the Vikings decided they could not continue, and sailed away.

Native American club with a wooden handle and stone head

VIKINGS GO EAST

It is not very far from the coast of Sweden to Russia, so it is not surprising that the Swedish Vikings went there, as the large number of Russian coins found in Sweden shows. The Swedish Vikings traveled inland along the rivers, following the Dnieper to the Black Sea and the Volga to the Caspian Sea.

Other Vikings journeyed southeast as far as the Byzantine Empire, which was all that remained of the old Roman Empire. Here, in the Byzantine capital of Constantinople, some of the Vikings became part of the Varangian Guard — the emperor's bodyguard.

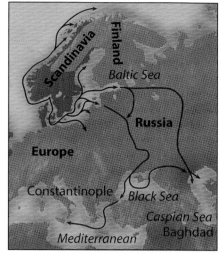

SAILING EAST

The Baltic Sea was a highway for ships bound for the coasts and rivers of Russia, and for those sailing along the coast of Scandinavia to Finland.

EASTERN RAIDS

Swedish Vikings raided along the coast and down the rivers of Russia, attacking any weak settlements, but trading too. They expanded trading at Kiev and Novgorod, which became large centers. When the rivers ended, the Vikings traveled on foot or by camel to Baghdad, Constantinople, and Jerusalem.

VIKING HORSEMEN

Viking clothes and equipment were influenced by the countries to which they traveled. This Swedish Viking's clothes, in particular the baggy legs of his trousers and a buttoned tunic, are central Asian in style. His horse has a Hungarian harness — the Hungarians were famous as fine horsemen.

Eastern Viking horseman

TRADE IN THE EAST

SILVER LOCKET
This locket, from a grave at Birka, Sweden, may have been an amulet full of spices. The design shows the "tree of life," and probably came from the Volga region or Baghdad.

PERSIAN BRAZIER
Traveling overland, Vikings visited Asia either as raiders or merchants. This brazier is just one of the many objects they brought back. Aromatic spices were also popular.

BRONZE BUDDHA
This religious statuette, found in the town of Helg, Sweden, was made in northern India in the 6th or 7th century. It was probably used by Vikings as an ornament.

RUS WARRIOR
The Swedish Vikings traveled and raided overland, unlike the Norwegian and Danish Vikings, who went by sea.

It is possible that Russia is named after the Swedish Vikings, because the local Slavs called them "Rus."

The Swedish Vikings often adopted Slav or central Asian equipment, such as the helmet with a pointed tip and baggy trousers gathered at the knees.

Arab and Byzantine writers give good descriptions of these peoples, and of their rather unclean habits. These included spitting in a communal washing bowl.

Rus warrior wearing central Asian-style helmet and trousers

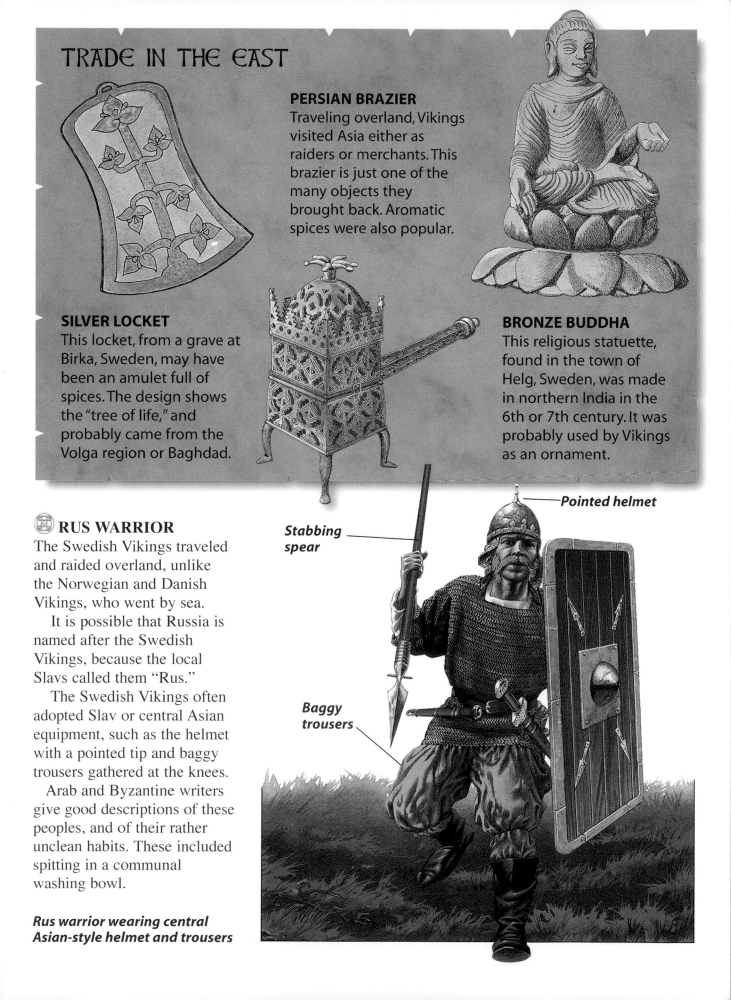

Stabbing spear

Pointed helmet

Baggy trousers

Battle Gods

The Vikings worshiped a number of gods and goddesses, but some were especially connected with battle. Odin was the god of the dead, feared because he could give victory or defeat. Those warriors who died in battle were welcomed into Odin's hall, Valhalla, which represented the grave and the underworld.

Thor was the sky god, the thunderer. Armed with his mighty hammer Mjöllnir, Thor protected Asgard, the home of the gods. His main enemy was the World Serpent, which lay coiled around the earth.

THROWING THE SPEAR
To win Odin's help before battle, a Viking warrior often symbolically sacrificed his enemies to the god. To do this he threw a javelin over them.

TALISMEN

Thor's hammer

THOR
This little figure from Iceland was made about 1000 and represents Thor seated and holding his hammer. Thor was usually described as a red-bearded god and is sometimes shown riding a chariot pulled by goats.

Bronze figure of Thor

THOR'S HAMMER
Many Vikings wore a hammer amulet, hoping it would give them protection. This one combines a Christian cross with Thor's hammer — the owner was taking no chances!

RAGNARÖK STONE
This carving shows Odin being eaten by his old enemy, the wolf Fenrir. In the sagas, the destruction of the gods (Ragnarök) and the last battle with giants and monsters follows.

THE VALKYRIE

In the first Viking sagas, the Valkyrie were fierce female spirits attending Odin. In later sagas, they are described as warrior maidens, princesses in armor riding on horseback over land and sea. They flew over battlefields to choose which dead warriors they should escort to Valhalla, where they were welcomed with horns of mead (a drink made from fermented honey).

SHIP BURIAL

A Viking chieftain was sometimes buried in a ship, to take him to the afterlife with his possessions. Slaves, horses, and other animals might be killed to accompany him. An Arab traveler described a Rus leader being buried in this way. In this case the ship was also burned so that the leader went to paradise quickly. A mound of earth was then raised over the ashes. Several ship burials have been discovered by archaeologists.

VALHALLA AND CHRISTIANITY

The old northern gods — such as Odin and Thor — had been worshiped by many Germanic peoples in Europe, but by the time of the Vikings, most of these peoples had become Christian. At first the Vikings regarded churches and monasteries as good places to plunder. In the 10th century, however, Viking kings began to help Christian missionaries, believing this would increase their own power.

The first Viking country to become Christian was Denmark in the 960s, under King Harald Bluetooth. Norway under King Olaf Haraldsson converted in about 1024, but Sweden remained pagan until the end of the 11th century.

CONVERSIONS
After Alfred the Great's defeat of the Danish leader Guthrum, in 878, the latter agreed to be baptized. The scene from an altar piece (right) shows a bishop baptizing Harald Bluetooth in a barrel.

VALHALLA
The Vikings believed that in Valhalla, warriors fought all day and then spent all evening and much of the night feasting with Odin. The god was said to collect the best warriors to help the gods in their last great battle with the monsters and giants.

CHRISTIANITY
Once ordinary people realized that their kings were not punished by the old gods for becoming Christian, they also converted to Christianity. Many fine wooden churches were built throughout Scandinavia.

The Vikings' carvings of Christ on the cross often show a proud and defiant figure — just like their old gods — rather than the usual suffering one.

CHRISTIAN SYMBOLS

STAVE CHURCH
Wooden churches, like this late 12th-century one that survives at Borgund in Norway, were built from tree trunks split in two (called staves). Early churches had only one story.

THE JELLING STONE
After becoming a Christian, King Harald Bluetooth put up this stone at Jelling in Jutland, Denmark, in memory of his parents, buried nearby. The 10th-century stone is the earliest known picture of Christ in Scandinavia.

THE URNES STYLE
Craftworkers carved the wooden panels of the 12th-century stave church at Urnes in Norway with ribbon-like beasts biting one another. The Vikings liked vigorous decoration, often using it on Christian buildings and objects.

 NORMAN KNIGHTS

In 911 a Viking called Rollo was given land in northwest France. His followers (known as Northmen or Normans) learned French, became Christians, and fought on horseback like French knights.

In 1066 Rollo's descendant, Duke William of Normandy, won the Battle of Hastings and conquered England.

Norman knight, descendant of Viking seafarers

 KNIGHTS ON HORSEBACK

Throughout the 12th century the Vikings gradually adopted the kind of equipment used in much of western and central Europe. Christian knights were trained to fight from horseback, tucking spears under their arms for the charge. They carried long kite-shaped shields instead of circular ones.

GLOSSARY

Amber
Golden- or orange-colored sap that seeps from pine trees and then solidifies. The Vikings used it for jewelry.

Asgard
The home of the gods.

Berserkir
Warrior who wore a bearskin shirt and fought in a frenzy.

Boss
Central iron dome in a shield to protect the hand holding it.

Byzantine Empire
In the 3rd century A.D. the Roman Empire was divided into eastern and western parts. The eastern part became the Byzantine Empire with its capital at Constantinople (modern Istanbul).

Caulking
Method of making boats watertight by sealing the spaces between the planks with shredded, tarred rope.

Clinker-built
Way of building boats in which the planks of the vessel overlap downward.

Danegeld
A kind of ransom paid to invading Danish armies so they would go away.

Danelaw
An area roughly north and east of a diagonal line across England, in which the Danes under Guthrum agreed to stay after making a treaty with King Alfred in 886.

Danish Great Army
The Viking force that attacked western Europe between 865 and 896, so called because of the number of men involved.

Dendrochronology
A way of dating wood, and objects made from wood, by counting the annual growth rings in the timber.

Fjord
Long narrow inlet of sea between high cliffs. Much of the coast of Norway is made up of fjords.

Franks
A Germanic people who controlled much of western Europe from the 6th century A.D. They eventually settled in what we now know as France and Germany.

Keel
The long timber running under a ship from front (bow) to rear (stern), to which the rest of the ship's structure is attached.

Knorr
Viking ship with deeper sides and fewer oars than a long ship, designed for carrying goods and trading.

Lindisfarne
Monastery off the northeast coast of England, famous for learning and, in 793, the first to be attacked by Vikings.

Lith
Group of warriors loyal to their chieftain.

Long ship
Slim, shallow-hulled ship designed for speed, with a single square sail. Long ships usually had at least thirteen rowers on each side.

Mjöllnir
Thor's magic hammer, with which he protected Asgard.

Odin
The god of death and the grave, who hung on a tree for three days to gain wisdom.

Pagan
Someone who has religious beliefs but does not follow one of the main world religions. In Viking times it meant a non-Christian.

Ragnarök
The doom of the gods, when their last great battle with the monsters and giants took place.

Runes
Ancient alphabet used by the peoples of Scandinavia before and during the Viking period. The letters were very angular, which made them easy to carve on stone and other hard materials.

Rus
Vikings from Sweden who settled in Russia and may have given the country its name.

Sagas
Long, epic tales of the bravery and outstanding deeds of legendary Viking heroes. Sagas, which were originally oral and were told by the skalds, were not written down until at least the 11th century, when the Vikings had become more settled.

Skalds
Viking poets and entertainers who specialized in reciting the sagas and other tales about the Vikings' gods and legendary heroes.

Skraelings
The Vikings' name for the native peoples they found in North America. It means "savages."

Spar
Thick pole used by the Vikings in their sails to help them steer.

Stave church
An early type of Scandinavian church in which logs are split in two and set upright side by side to form the walls.

Steering oar
Large oar attached near the rear right end of a Viking ship and used for steering, instead of the more usual central rudder.

Thor
The god of thunder. A popular god whose protection was sought by both warriors and farmers. His symbol, and magic weapon, was a hammer.

Thrall
A slave, often a captive taken by the Vikings in battle or during a raid.

Ulfhednar
"Wolfskin-clad one." A warrior who wore a wolfskin and, like the *berserkir*, fought in a frenzy.

Valhalla
The mythical hall of Odin, to which chosen heroes were brought after their death in battle or sacrifice. It sometimes meant life after death.

Valkyries
Female servants of Odin who chose which of the warriors killed in battle should be taken to Valhalla to be with Odin. Once feared as demons, the Valkyries came to be regarded as princesses in armor who rode through the skies on magnificent warhorses.

Varangian Guard
The Viking warriors who served the Byzantine emperor at Constantinople and formed his bodyguard.

Vinland
"Wineland." The Vikings' name for the area on the northeast coast of North America where they settled. Archaeologists think it is likely to have been Newfoundland in Canada. The "vines" were probably the huckleberries that grow there and not real grape vines.

INDEX